# Welcome Home

A heartwarming housewarming book filled
with tips, recipes, and stories
about home.

*From Life Point Books™.*

# WELCOME HOME

First published 2023 by Good Stories Publishing, LLC.
Copyright © Good Stories Publishing, LLC., 2023.

All rights reserved. No part of this book may be reprinted or reproduced and utilized in any form by any electronic, mechanical or other means, not known or hereafter invested without permission in writing from the publishers.

Library of Congress Control Number: 2022923530
Library of Congress Cataloging-in-publication Data
Welcome Home.

Welcome Home.
Life Point Books™.
By: Marlene Byrne
ISBN: 978-1-7370092-3-8

The stories, recipes, and tips in this book are not original but rather handed down by people who found their house and made it a "home." Please check your product owner's manuals and other directions when doing any repairs or maintenance in your home.

## DEDICATION

This book was inspired by my nieces and nephews -

Megan, Bridget, Patrick, Clare, and Brendan.

As they started new lives in their first homes,

I wanted to find a special gift.

This is for them.

# REMEMBER THE MOMENT

Address of your new home:
_____

Moved from:
_____

Moved in (date):
_____

The weather on move-in day was:

🟠 Sunny    🟣 Rainy    ⚪ Snowy    🟡 Warm    🔵 Cold    ⚪ Cloudy

Names of friends and/or family who helped move:
_____
_____

Describe the first night spent in your new home:
_____
_____
_____
_____

## REMEMBER THE MOMENT

New discoveries about your new home:
_____
_____
_____


Favorite thing in your new home:
_____
_____
_____


First meal in your new home:
_____

# FINDING WHAT YOU NEED

**Remember the Moment**   v

**Introduction**   x

**GOOD STORIES**

1. A Chicago Knocker, My Story   1
2. In the Walls   7
3. Rooftop Party   13
4. Secret Hiding Place   21
5. House with a Dog   27
6. Add Water   33
7. Holiday Tree Trip   41
8. Stewards of the House for Now   51
9. Write Your Good Story   61

**HOUSE NOTES**

Unpacking Tips   3
Safety Tips   9
Organization Tips   15
Security Tips   23
Maintenance Tips   29
Neighborhood Community Tips   35
Decorating Tips   43
Entertaining Tips   53
Backyard Party Tips   63

**RECIPES**

| | |
|---|---|
| Sandwiches and Snacks | 5 |
| Crockpot Shredded Chicken | 11 |
| Simple Coleslaw | 11 |
| Lasagna | 17 |
| Honey Carrots | 18 |
| Chicken Pasta e Fagioli Soup | 25 |
| Veggie Fish Bake | 31 |
| Chicken Pot Pie | 37 |
| Simple Salad | 38 |
| Steaks on the Grill | 47 |
| Roasted Garlic Potatoes | 48 |
| Cranberry Walnut Salad | 49 |
| Beef Tenderloin | 56 |
| Flaky Potatoes | 57 |
| Roasted Broccoli and Cauliflower | 58 |
| Salty Beef Dip | 65 |
| Charcuterie Board | 66 |
| Brats and Onions | 67 |
| Lily Lake Beans | 68 |
| Pooky Pasta Salad | 69 |
| Special K® Peanut Butter Bars | 70 |
| Margarita Heaven | 71 |

## CONGRATULATIONS ON YOUR NEW HOME

Because this book was probably a gift, I'm assuming someone in your life is excited about your new home adventure. They love you enough to try to find that perfect gift to celebrate this special life moment. I hope the stories, tips, and recipes exceed those expectations and provide a few treasures to help you start the journey from house to home.

This book includes a fun collection of stories about others who have stepped across the threshold of their new house. Like you, they were anxious to start new traditions and build family memories in this wonderful place we call home.

Highlighting ideas for nine meals, *Welcome Home* is meant to be a practical guide, from unpacking to decorating to entertaining. In these pages, you will find a series of tips on things to manage your house. Recipes to help make eating together a part of the journey. And those crazy, interesting stories of people who found "home."

As the years pass, this place will reflect your milestones and what family means to you. There may be pets. Children. Traditions. Parties. And even sorrow. Through it all, this will be the place you dream, find comfort, take refuge, and eventually, where you will reminisce.

Be nourished in your new surroundings. Appreciate all the hard work. Be happy. Be together. Be home.

Marlene Byrne

## A CHICAGO KNOCKER, MY STORY

*By: Marlene Byrne*

When my husband and I started searching for our first home in Chicago, there were so many duds. I remember a listing that highlighted a "huge" deck. When we toured the house, the deck was about 10x10 feet. Hardly huge by any standard. The market was tight, the costs were high, and we were becoming discouraged.

One Sunday afternoon, we walked up to a house, and before ringing the doorbell, we noticed the knocker on the front door. There, engraved in the metal, was our last name. Our realtor was late, and the owners — an older couple — invited us in. We introduced ourselves and had a lovely laugh at the coincidence of having the same last name.

The couple started to show us the house. As we became acquainted, they shared tales of raising four children in the neighborhood — the parties, the holidays, the laughter. You could almost visualize the fun they had shared as a family. Obviously nostalgic, they were empty nesters and felt it was time to downsize.

*The feeling of being "home" was almost immediate. We were delighted when they accepted our offer.*

The moving truck couldn't arrive until the day after the closing, but we were so excited, we slept on an air mattress in the empty living room. When we arrived at the house, there was a gift basket on the kitchen counter with champagne and a note from the couple.

"We hope your family grows with love in this house just like ours did. The door knocker is yours to keep. Welcome home."

Our first night was spent talking about the future.

A few years later, we ran into the couple. By this time, we had two children, and they were delighted we were raising our family in "their" home. They happily confessed that they had another offer but felt we were the right couple to carry on the house's tradition of happiness.

# House Notes

UNPACKING TIPS

### 1. Mark Your Boxes
As you pack or as the boxes come off the truck, mark each by room and number them by importance. It will help make unpacking much more manageable. You can tackle things one box at a time or push a box to the side for another day.

### 2. Clean While You Wait
Arrive at the house with cleaning supplies. Make sure they're easily accessible in your car, not packed up in boxes, so you can bring them into the house first. If the moving truck shows up a bit late, it will allow you to get a head start while you wait.

### 3. Unpack Second
Place boxes in the center of each room. Ask anyone who has lived in their home for a long time about the last time they got behind a heavy dresser or moved the bed to scrub the floor. This is an opportunity to clean while the rooms are empty or at least uncluttered. Clean before you unpack and then place the dresser in its perfect spot.

### 4. Bedroom First
Start by cleaning your bedroom and set up this room first. After the exertion of moving, you will need to rest. Locating the sheets and blankets, making the bed, and being ready to tuck in that first night will feel great after a long day.

### 5. Determine Garbage Day
Most communities recycle but not all pick up on the same day. You will inevitably have loads of boxes to recycle so make sure you find out the days and rules for both garbage and recycling pickup. Many recycling companies want boxes broken down to minimize space in their trucks.

## SIMPLE FOOD

The first day in any new house is chaotic. It is not a day for recipe advice, so I am not going to give you any. I want to talk about convenience and recommend keeping the menu simple while remembering you may have bodies to feed. Instead of a recipe, I am offering a grocery list to send with a friend or family member to the nearest store. Everyone will want to help you. Let them. Feeding the troops is important if you have help with moving and unpacking.

*(Ingredient lists in this book are designed to take a quick picture on your phone before running to the store.)*

## SANDWICHES AND SNACKS

I love the idea of having a bowl of fruit and beverages available for the moving crew. They can grab a banana or grapes on their way to and from the truck. When lunch comes around, you can serve simple sandwiches and salads. Either buy ready-made sandwiches or the ingredients for guests to make their own. Everyone will be happy and nourished as they continue their afternoon tasks.

**INGREDIENTS:**

Fruit including grapes, apples, berries, and bananas
Lemonade, iced tea, or other drinks
Chips
Potato salad or other deli salad options

*If not ready-made:*

Bread (anything you like but I prefer a fresh loaf sliced by the bakery)

*Head to the deli for these ingredients:*

Turkey, sliced
Roast beef, sliced
Muenster cheese, sliced
Pepperjack cheese, sliced
Pickles
Tomato
Margarine or butter
Mustard, mayonnaise, or other condiments

# Good Story 2

## IN THE WALLS

*By: Sandy B.*

I love older homes. The details. The stories. Even the creaky floors. There's a special charm to all that history.

When it was time for our family to upgrade, my husband and I decided to find something with character. As we walked through what would become our house, the realtor told us how it was built. The house was a mail-order home from the Sears, Roebuck, and Co. catalog. These houses were called "Sears Modern Homes" and sold as kit houses in the early 1900s.

This house was built in 1910 and still had many of the original features. A beautiful stone fireplace, a large front porch, and plaster archways between the rooms. We intuitively knew it was "home."

Note: From 1908 to 1942, Sears sold more than 70,000 houses primarily through mail order. Sears Modern Homes offered more than 370 designs in a wide range of architectural styles and sizes over the line's 34-year history. Primarily shipped via railroad boxcars, these kits included most of the materials needed to build the house. Once delivered, many of these homes were assembled by the new homeowner, relatives, and friends, in a fashion like the traditional barn-raisings common in farming communities.

We planned to move into the house and immediately renovate the kitchen. While demolishing a kitchen wall, my husband, John, discovered the original receipt for the purchase of the home taped to a joist inside the wall. At 112 years old, discovering the receipt was like finding a time capsule.

We carefully pressed the receipt between two pieces of paper. Later, we had it framed to hang as artwork in our new kitchen.

The discovery gave me an idea as we continued the remodeling project. Along with our children, we created a time capsule and placed it behind the drywall of the new construction. Someday, another family will discover the contents and be able to reminisce about the rich history of this house.

> We intuitively knew it was "home."

SAFETY TIPS

### 1. Test the Smoke Detectors
I love interconnected smoke alarms because if one sounds, they all sound. Most important is to ensure your detectors — no matter which type — are functional. Insert new batteries as soon as you move in, then test smoke alarms monthly and change alkaline batteries at least once a year. Set a reminder in your phone or pick a holiday as your yearly "battery" day.

### 2. Confirm the Carbon Monoxide Detectors
Carbon monoxide is a dangerous gas that is colorless and odorless. CO detectors are the only way to know if carbon monoxide is affecting the air quality in your home and an important way to detect exposure. They should be placed in your home to help prevent serious illness and even death. Test the detectors monthly to ensure they are working properly. Refer to the user manual for instructions to test your specific model.

### 3. Find Your Electrical Panel
The electrical panel (generally a circuit breaker unless you own an older home, which may still have a fuse box) distributes electricity throughout your home. It's important to become familiar with how your electricity is distributed, because operating too many devices on a single circuit or fuse can cause an overload. For example, turning on a microwave, hairdryer, and lights all at the same time may result in an overloaded circuit or fuse. If this happens and you have a circuit breaker, unplug one or more of the offending devices, switch the breaker off and then back on. If you have fuses, you'll need to replace the fuse. It's good to have fuses of various ratings on hand. Find a licensed electrician you can contact if you have ongoing electrical issues or questions about your electrical panel.

### 4. Locate the Main Water Shutoff
The main water shutoff valve is located inside your home, typically on a perimeter wall where the water enters your house. If you have a water leak or need to turn off the water for any reason, you'll need to know how to shut off this valve. Turning the valve to the right will shut off water to the entire house, even the outside spigots. Consider turning off the water when you're leaving on a long vacation or are going to be away for any substantial length of time to prevent potential leaks.

### 5. Change the Garage Door Code
When you move into a new home, one of your first tasks should be to change the garage door code. Directions for resetting the code based on your model should be in the owner's manual or on the Internet. And while you're at it, program the setting into your car if it has the capability.

## CROCK POT DAY

The smell in your house on day two will be just one of the advantages of crockpot cooking. Another advantage is the simple prep. Just add the ingredients and give it a stir every time you pass by throughout the day.

# Let's Eat

## CROCKPOT SHREDDED CHICKEN

**INGREDIENTS:**

1 ½ cups Sweet Baby Ray's® BBQ Sauce
½ medium onion, sliced
1 T. olive oil
1 T. Worcestershire sauce
2 T. brown sugar
3 lbs. boneless chicken breasts
(trim the fat)
Buns
Bag of chips

**DIRECTIONS:**

Add the first five ingredients to a 5-quart (or larger) slow cooker and stir well. Place in chicken and turn to coat. Cover and turn the crockpot on high for 4 hours (6-7 hours on low). Then 30 minutes before serving, pull out chicken pieces and shred them on a cutting board, pulling them apart with two forks. Place shredded chicken back in the sauce and stir. Cook on low for the last 30 minutes so the sauce soaks into the chicken.

Serve on fresh buns. I love to serve it with coleslaw and salty chips. You can buy coleslaw at the deli or try this easy recipe.

Serves 4-6 people.

## SIMPLE COLESLAW

**INGREDIENTS:**

*Dressing:*
½ cup mayonnaise
1 T. white vinegar
½ T. cider vinegar
2 tsp. sugar
½ tsp. celery seeds
Salt & pepper to taste

*Greens:*
3 cups green cabbage, finely shredded
2 cups purple cabbage, finely shredded
1 large carrot, finely shredded

**DIRECTIONS:**

Stir together all ingredients to combine. Refrigerate at least one hour before serving.

Serves 4-6 people.

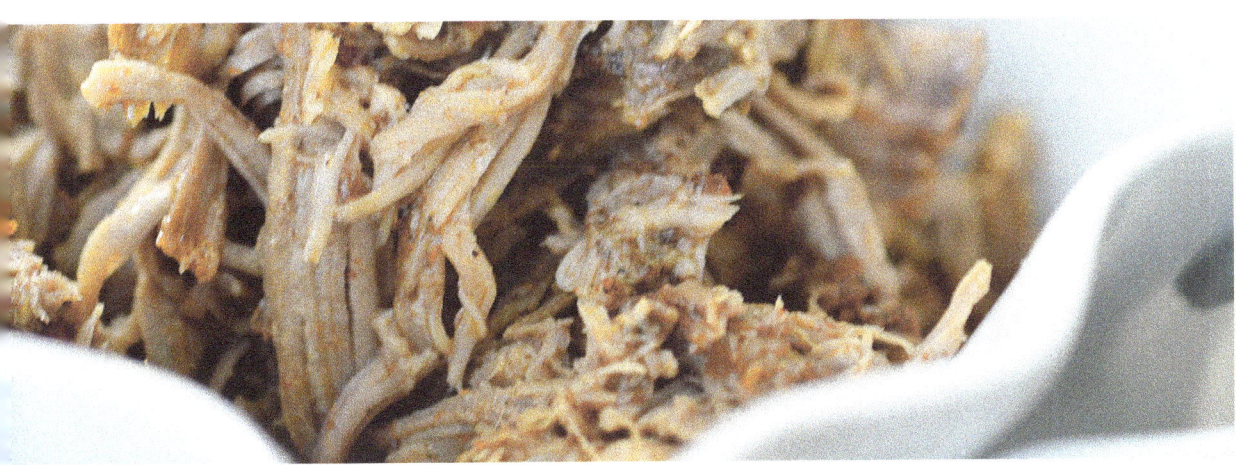

# Good Story

## ROOFTOP PARTY

*By: Bob A.*

John and I were renting in the city and looking for a downtown condominium. As a doctor, I wanted to be close to the hospital and was excited to find a new listing for a condominium in the perfect location. The selling realtor was throwing an open house party the following Sunday afternoon to generate interest in the unit. We were worried about missing out on the opportunity and arrived early to the event.

We arrived at the condo at 1:00pm on the dot. We were the first to arrive and found the realtor in the kitchen, bleeding. She had cut her arm on an exit door to the rooftop deck while setting up for the party and was trying to control the bleeding before everyone arrived.

John went to our car to retrieve my emergency kit while I moved her to the bathroom to work on controlling the bleeding. The cut was quite deep, and I was worried about her fainting, so I sat her on the seat in the shower. As I tended to her wound and John helped, we found ourselves all in the shower together.

*The realtor, who had quite a personality, said, "Think about how roomy this shower is. Three people can easily fit inside."*

After the laughing stopped, John and I took our first glimpse of the beautiful bathroom and were immediately sold. Nicknaming it a "blood sale," we made our offer and confirmed the purchase of the property the next day.

# House Notes

ORGANIZATION TIPS

### 1. Make Spare Keys
No one ever plans to lose their house key, but you'll be glad to have an extra if you do. Many hardware stores duplicate keys either by hand or with automated machines. Take a key with you when you make one of the inevitable runs to the hardware store and make 3-4 duplicates. Don't forget to label them and place them in a designated drawer so you can retrieve them later.

### 2. Designate a "Key" Spot
As you establish routines in your new home, determine where you (and that's all of you) will put your keys. Make it a habit to put them in the same place every time. That way, you always know where they are for ease and convenience, especially on those days when you're in a hurry and can't afford even a few seconds to look for them. If you have small children, place them out of reach, maybe on hooks that only the adults can reach.

### 3. Share a Key
I recommend sharing a key with a friend or trusted new neighbor. In the event you need someone to check on your house or you find yourself standing outside without a key, you can contact your trusted keyholder and gain entry. It's also great if you have a dog and find yourself in an emergency. You can contact your keyholder for a doggie favor.

### 4. Post Office Change of Address
You can change your address on the USPS website (www.usps.com). It offers mail forwarding as well as a change of address for your voter registration. Simply fill out the fields and submit them to the post office. I recommend introducing yourself to the mail carrier and letting them know you are new to the neighborhood.

### 5. Update Your Address
Don't forget to change your address with friends, family, and delivery services. Email your new address to friends and family. As your forwarded mail comes in, reach out to update your address to any entity that still has the old one.

## PASTA DAY IS HERE

By now the moving crew has gone home. There is peace to having the house to yourselves even if there's still work to be done. I love lasagna because it's easy to prep ahead and bake when ready to eat. It's also a chance for a sit-down meal together.

# Let's  Eat

## LASAGNA

### INGREDIENTS:

2 lbs. lean ground beef  
Garlic salt  
Oregano  
Salt  
Pepper  

No-cook lasagna noodles  
45 oz. Ragu® traditional sauce  
16 oz. cottage cheese  
4 cups pkg. shredded mozzarella  
Baguette bread  

### DIRECTIONS:

Brown the ground beef and drain thoroughly. Set on a paper towel to soak up any excess grease. Place noodles in a single layer in a 9x13 metal or glass pan. Sprinkle on half the browned ground beef. Spoon half the cottage cheese in dollops and spread it into the ground beef. Pour half the Ragu® and sprinkle with garlic salt, oregano, salt, and pepper. Sprinkle on half of the mozzarella. Place another layer of noodles and repeat the entire process, topping with the remaining mozzarella. You can make it ahead of time and put it in the refrigerator.

Preheat the oven to 350 degrees.

Bake for 40 minutes until the cheese is bubbling and lightly brown. Remove from the oven and let stand 15 minutes before cutting into squares. I love to serve it with fresh bread. Add a vegetable if you have time. The honey carrot recipe on the next page is an easy side dish.

Serves 6 people. If you are only serving two, you can split the ingredients into two smaller pans and freeze one batch or enjoy leftovers for lunch. Make sure to tightly seal it if freezing.

# HONEY CARROTS

**INGREDIENTS:**

1 lb. carrots
2 T. butter
2 T. honey
1 T. lemon juice
Salt
Pepper

**DIRECTIONS:**

Wash carrots, remove/peel skin, and slice into 2-inch pieces.

In a medium saucepan on the stovetop, add the sliced carrots and sprinkle with salt. Add enough water to cover and then bring to a boil.

Boil until tender — about 6 minutes. Drain and put back into the pan. Add butter, honey, and lemon juice. Sauté on low for about 5 minutes, stirring until glaze forms and coats the carrots. Season with salt and pepper and serve.

Serves 4-6 people.

# Good 4 Story

## SECRET HIDING PLACE

*By: Connie D.*

Matt and I were moving to a larger home with our three kids. Our youngest son, MJ, was finding the move difficult. Besides the fact that his best friend lived two houses away in the old neighborhood, he was not great at handling change.

Our new house had four bedrooms. To try to make the move bearable, I told each of the kids they could decorate their bedroom with anything they wanted. No questions asked. I hoped it would make the move fun and create comfortable spaces that felt all their own.

MJ could not decide what to do in his room. I believed it was the anxiety about the move that caused his resistance. While his siblings were decorating their spaces, he was simply unpacking. He told us he would pick a theme later.

Up in his room one afternoon, MJ was lying on the carpet, tossing his football in the air, when he noticed the baseboard in the corner was crooked. He sat on the floor and pulled on the wood with his fingernails. To his surprise, a section of the board pulled open and a hole in the drywall appeared.

*He had discovered the secret hiding place of the last occupant.*

It was the inspiration he needed to find his bedroom theme. At first, he was afraid to tell me about the spot for fear Matt and I might want to secure the molding. Instead, he announced the theme of his bedroom as a Spy Zone. My husband loves James Bond, and I immediately looked at him. He shook his head and said, "It wasn't me."

MJ confessed to finding the hiding space to Matt as they were searching the Internet for spy decor. They made a pact to keep the secret from everyone else in the family. It also allowed my husband to introduce MJ to the classic 007 films.
MJ used the hiding spot to keep things out of reach of his siblings for years. We credit the secret spot with helping him adjust to our new home.

> To his surprise, a section of the board pulled open...

# House Notes

SECURITY TIPS

### 1. Lock the Windows
For windows on the first floor, it is especially important to make sure they are securely locked. Bad guys prey on easy targets, and an unlocked window offers quick entry. Make sure to check things are locked, especially when you are going away.

### 2. Light it Up
Keep the front porch light on or add lighting to the outside of your home to make things visible. If you park a car outside or on the street, lighting up the area helps deter thieves.

### 3. Stranger Danger
Be careful when you answer the door and don't allow just anyone into your home. If you didn't ask them to come to your home, assume they probably don't belong there.

### 4. Lock Up the Car
Always lock your cars and make sure to remove any valuables, especially if they're parked outside.

### 5. 'Ring' the Door
I love interactive doorbells with video options. They are a great housewarming gift and offer the option of seeing who is at your door from your phone. Some options let you talk, and others even capture real-time video of who is on the porch — all without opening the door.

## TIME FOR SOUP

Soup is always a great meal for comfort and nourishment. I call this soup "one for the soul." It's a hearty soup with veggies and pasta, making it a meal. The recipe can be made even easier by purchasing a pre-cooked rotisserie chicken, available at most grocery stores. I like to serve it with fresh bread and fruit to take care of all the food groups.

## CHICKEN PASTA e FAGIOLI SOUP

### INGREDIENTS:

2 T. olive oil
¾ lb. Swiss chard, chopped
1 ¼ cup onion, diced
1 ¼ cup carrots, sliced
2 tsp. fresh rosemary, chopped
1 tsp. garlic, minced
¼ tsp. crushed red pepper flakes
5 cups chicken broth, reduced sodium

1 (28 oz. can) diced tomatoes
1 (16 oz. can) kidney beans, drained not rinsed
3 cups roasted chicken (I buy a rotisserie chicken at the store and dice the breasts.)
1 ¼ cup ditalini pasta
2 T. parmesan cheese, grated
Fresh bread

### DIRECTIONS:

Chop 1 cup of the red Swiss chard stems. Dice the onions. Peel and slice the carrots. Chop the fresh rosemary and mince the garlic. Open all the cans.

Chop 4 cups of the Swiss chard, removing the hard veins. Cut the chicken breasts into bite-size pieces.

Heat oil in a soup pot. Add the Swiss chard stems, onions, carrots, rosemary, garlic, and red pepper flakes. Sauté for 5 minutes. Add Swiss chard leaves and sauté for 2 minutes. Add broth, tomatoes and kidney beans, and bring to a boil. Reduce heat to low and cover for 10 minutes.

Stir in chicken and pasta and bring to a boil and then reduce heat to low, cover and simmer for 10 minutes. Ladle into bowls and top with grated Parmesan cheese.

Serve with fresh Italian bread. Enjoy.

Serves 4-6 people. When I make for just two of us, I boil a small amount of noodles separately and spoon them into my soup bowls at each meal.

# Good Story 5

## HOUSE WITH A DOG

*By: Tim S.*

Nancy and I were moving to a small town and bought our new house from a couple moving to the country. They had lived in town while their children were young and in school but now, as empty nesters, they wanted to move back out into the country.

*The house was perfect. It had three bedrooms, an open kitchen, and a family room. It also had a big, fenced-in backyard which was perfect for our three young children.*

On moving day, while unloading the van, I heard a small dog barking at my feet. There was a little beagle. We had met the dog, named Luna, at the open house. The dog wagged its tail and headed for the front door, which was propped open. She marched right in and went to the kitchen to find Nancy unpacking. It was obvious, the dog was simply coming home.

That afternoon, following a phone call, the previous owners came to pick up Luna and take her back to their country house.

While drinking coffee the next morning, I heard the barking again. I opened the front door and there was Luna, sitting on the porch. The kids came running to see the dog. Someone yelled out, "Can we keep her?"

This time, Nancy and the kids took her to the living room to play while I called Luna's owners. They apologized profusely and came to retrieve the dog again.

On day three, Luna arrived at lunchtime. Nancy told the owners not to rush to get her. The kids loved her visits, and they could stop in to get her any time. It was obvious Luna considered this her home.

From then on, when Luna visited, our calls to the owners would delay her retrieval so the kids had time to play. We soon became friends with Luna's parents, and she became part of our family. When Luna's family went out of town, Nancy and I volunteered the kids to take care of her. Luna got her wish, and a bowl with her name on it placed in both kitchens.

*It was obvious, the dog was simply coming home.*

# House Notes

## MAINTENANCE TIPS

### 1. Check the Furnace Filter
Furnace filters trap particles pulled through your cold air ducts and route the filtered air into your home through the heat exchanger. If they are not regularly changed, it not only affects the air quality in your home, but also the air flow to your vents. When replacing your filter, make sure you determine the proper type for your furnace model. Every furnace has a different filter thickness which determines the replacement frequency, so check your furnace model.

### 2. Close the Flue
If your new home has a fireplace, ensure the flue is closed to prevent warm air from escaping up the chimney. You should open the damper before lighting a fire and close it once the fire is completely burned out and the area has cooled. Be careful cleaning your fireplace as embers can be hot long after the fire is extinguished.

### 3. Light Up Right
Check all light sources in your new home and update to energy-efficient models, which last up to 12 times longer than traditional bulbs. They also use less electricity while emitting the same amount of light. Their energy efficiency helps reduce your electric bill and will make you feel good about reducing your carbon footprint.

### 4. Is That a Drip?
Sinks, toilets, outdoor spouts, and laundry rooms are all places to check for dripping water. These drips can add up to expensive water bills. You can test for leaks by checking the water meter. Have everyone refrain from using faucets or flushing the toilets, turn off all water sources, and wait for 15 minutes. Check your water meter to see if it is running. If it is, you know you have a leak somewhere. Find the dripping faucet or running toilet and put it on your repair list.

### 5. Let the Air Flow
Every clothes dryer vents air through a large tube. These vents exit the house and typically have a cap or flap. Make sure lint and other fuzz have not built up over time and clogged the tube. To clean the dryer duct, open the interior flap and remove lint by hand and then vacuum the inside of the duct. Use hose extensions, if available, to vacuum out as much of the duct as you can. Go outside the house and remove the exterior vent cover to check for lint as well.

## DELICIOUS AND NUTRITIOUS

This recipe takes some time to prepare (think chopping) but it's easy and super healthy. You can cut the veggies and prep the fish in advance, wrapping everything in tinfoil and putting items in the refrigerator until 15 minutes before serving. I have included the recipe with four filets, but you can easily reduce the veggies and make it for two people.

# Let's  Eat

## VEGGIE FISH BAKE

### INGREDIENTS:

8 small red potatoes
2 carrots
4 oz. green beans
¼ cup olive oil
¼ cup soy sauce

1 large leek
2 green onions
4 fresh 6 oz. fish filets —
(Salmon, tilapia or any white fish you like)

2 T. fresh dill
1 T. fresh basil
1 T. butter
Non-stick cooking spray
Fresh bread

### DIRECTIONS:

As you chop, place each vegetable into a separate pile or bowl. Dice the potatoes. Peel and slice the carrots. Cut beans into 1-inch pieces. Slice the leek up to the pale green and chop it into pieces. Throw the green stem away. Slice the green onions up to the pale green. Throw the green stems away. Chop the fresh dill and basil into small pieces.

Use a frying pan with high sides to parboil the vegetables. Add ¼ inch of water to cover the bottom of the pan and then add butter and heat. Once boiling, add potatoes and cover for 5 minutes. Then add the carrots to the potatoes and cover for 3 minutes. Next, add the green beans and cover for 3 minutes. Drain any water from the mixture and add in leeks, onions, dill, and basil. Add olive oil and soy sauce. Season with salt and pepper. Stir carefully until the vegetables are coated.

Spray four long sheets of tinfoil with nonstick spray. Place the fish in the middle and spoon the veggie mixture evenly over the four filets. Top with a small pad of butter. Pull up the long edges of the tinfoil and seal it into a tent.

Preheat the oven to 450 degrees.

I put the tinfoil packages on a cookie sheet. Bake at 450 degrees for 20 minutes if vegetables are still warm (25 minutes if packets are cold). Let stand for 5 minutes when you remove it from the oven. Carefully open the end of the tinfoil and pour onto a plate.

Serve with fresh bread. Serves 4 people but can easily be adjusted as each packet is individual. Reduce or increase the vegetables and other ingredients as needed.

# Good Story

## ADD WATER

*By: Courtney D.*

I was pregnant when we were searching for our first house. Not just a *little* pregnant but almost eight months along. Steve and I knew we wanted a neighborhood with a good school and a house with room for our growing family. Things like a backyard and more than one bathroom were non-negotiable.

The realtor was showing us houses and one afternoon, we walked up to a brick house with a bright red front door. Inside we met a sweet little lady named Anna who was the current homeowner. She had raised her family there and now, as a widow, was moving closer to her adult children.

Anna wanted to hear everything about the upcoming baby. When was our due date? Did we know the sex? Did we have other children?

I explained this baby was our first and that the gender was going to be a surprise. Anna said she had three children and seven grandchildren. She politely asked if she could feel my belly.

As she placed her feeble hands on both sides of my growing stomach, she looked straight into my eyes. "I have one piece of advice if you want to hear it," she said.

"Of course!" I said.

**"When things get tough - and they will - put the baby in water. It doesn't matter if they sit in the sink, take a bath, or just play in the basin of the bathroom, water is a great relaxer. It works every time,"** Anna said. **"And take time to put yourself in a nice bath too."**

Steve and I went on to buy Anna's house. I delivered a baby boy, and we named him Michael. And every time we had an evening when he was fussy or a long Saturday afternoon with nothing to do, we put him in water. It worked just like Anna predicted and reminded us of her kind words.

# House Notes

## NEIGHBORHOOD + COMMUNITY TIPS

### 1. Neighborhood Watch

Introducing yourself to your new neighbors is a wonderful way to be, well, "neighborly." It's also a good safety measure. Neighbors who know each other tend to watch out for each other. When we moved into our first home, I made a map and wrote down everyone's names as we met them so I would not forget. It's a busy time and you might be asking, "What was their name again?" later.

### 2. Stay in Touch with Your Realtor

Good realtors live by their reputation and word of mouth. The realtor typically knows the area and can help if you have questions. They should have information about any neighborhood associations or where you can get a good plumber. Don't be afraid to call and use them as a resource for questions that arise.

### 3. Say Hello

Introduce yourself to delivery service providers (U.S. Mail, Amazon, UPS®, FedEx, etc.). Let them know you are new to the neighborhood.

### 4. What's Nearby?

If you are moving to a new location, it can be overwhelming to find your way around. Take a little time to locate area retailers and service providers: grocery stores, the bank, the post office, a pharmacy, and for sure a hardware store.

### 5. Build Community

No matter where you live, having a sense of community is important. Whether it's a church, a social group, or the health club, make sure to find ways to meet people. They will be great resources for the "best" pizza or a great dentist. When we moved to Chicago, I found our best recommendations came from neighbors and friends.

## TIME FOR COMFORT FOOD

Today I warm your heart with chicken pot pie. This is another recipe that can be made in the morning and kept in the refrigerator until ready to cook. It's a hearty meal with loads of vegetables, so if you want to pair it with anything, I recommend a simple salad or fruit.

# Let's Eat

## CHICKEN POT PIE

### INGREDIENTS:

2 T. olive oil
1 cup potatoes
(1 large or 2 medium)
1 cup onions
1 cup celery
1 cup carrots

⅓ cup butter
½ cup flour
2 cups chicken broth
1 cup half & half
1 tsp. salt

¼ tsp. pepper
4 cups diced chicken
2 pie crusts (Pillsbury™ has ready-made in the cold section of stores.)

### DIRECTIONS:

If you purchase raw chicken breasts, dice and cook them in a pan on the stove with your favorite seasonings. You can also purchase an already roasted rotisserie chicken and cut it into bite-sized pieces.

Set aside the diced, cooked chicken. Dice the potatoes. Slice celery. Peel and slice carrots. Chop the onion. Mix the broth with the half & half. Open and unroll the first pie crust and place it on the bottom of a glass pie pan. Preheat the oven to 400 degrees.

Heat butter in a frying pan with sides. Sauté onions, celery, carrots, and potatoes in butter for 10 minutes. Add flour to the mixture, stirring constantly for 1 minute until the veggies are coated.

Pour the combined broth and half & half slowly over the vegetable mixture. Stir and cook until thick. Take off the heat and add salt, pepper, and chicken. Pour the mixture into the pie crust. Do not overfill. Open the second pie crust, unroll, and place it on top. Seal around the edge with a fork and poke a few holes in the top.

Bake at 400 degrees for 45-50 minutes until the top is golden brown. Remove and let cool for 10-15 minutes before cutting. Add a simple salad (see the following page). Enjoy.

Serves 4-6 people.

## SIMPLE SALAD

**INGREDIENTS:**

1 ½ T. fresh lemon juice
1 ½ T. extra-virgin olive oil
¼ tsp. ground black pepper
⅛ tsp. kosher salt
1 tsp. Worcestershire sauce

6 cups mixed greens or baby spinach
1 cup cherry tomatoes, halved
⅓ cup onion, chopped
¼ cup Gorgonzola crumbles

**DIRECTIONS:**

Combine lemon juice, olive oil, pepper, salt, and Worcestershire sauce in a large bowl and whisk together. Add salad ingredients and toss to coat.

*Facts About Salts:*

In cooking, kosher salt and flaky sea salt can be used interchangeably. For most recipes, I recommend cooking with kosher salt because it is consistent. Sea salt is usually minimally processed, so it retains trace levels of nutrients like magnesium, iron, calcium, and potassium. Sea salt has a coarser grain than table salt and is softer than kosher salt so it's great on meat. It's notable for its crunchy texture and potent flavor.

# Good 7 Story

## HOLIDAY TREE TRIP

*By: Mary M.*

My husband, Charles, was promoted and relocated by his company. His start date was in January which meant switching schools mid-year for our children. The change would be good in the long run, but we knew our kids would miss their old neighborhood.

The kids could start their new school at the beginning of a semester, but they would still have to make new friends. To top things off, moving at Christmastime held its own set of challenges. I was fearful of disappointing the family by changing our holiday traditions.

Charles and I found a great house and set the move in date for December 20. The stress of the move, as well as staring into the faces of three disappointed children, was compounded by the pressures of Christmas gifts.

*We decided to reduce the number of gifts we bought the kids and added a family gift, a "special envelope" which we hung on the tree. Opening it together, they discovered our plans for a vacation to Disney at the end of the school year.*

After months of adjustment, the trip to Disney was the best vacation of our lives. In a conversation on the way home, Charles asked the kids, "Did you like the gift on our tree?"

Unanimously they said, "Yes."

Then he asked, "Do you remember any of your other gifts?"

They all looked at each other with puzzled faces. No one could remember one gift they had opened.

We called it the Christmas Tree Trip, and it became an annual tradition. Each year, Charles and I place a secret envelope on the tree and the kids open their adventure. The location has become part of the holiday anticipation and our trips have made memories for a lifetime.

*The Christmas Tree Trip became an annual tradition.*

# House Notes 7

## DECORATING TIPS

### 1. 'Greiges' are the Rage

Greige is a blend of gray and beige. It can be the best of both worlds, appealing to those that like the look of gray, but are not sure about moving away from the more traditional feeling of beige. Greiges make a great whole-house paint color choice because they tend to go with everything and appeal to everyone.

**EXAMPLE: *Benjamin Moore Revere Pewter (HC-172)***
Probably the most beloved greige paint color, it is no wonder designers love Revere Pewter. It has just the right mix of gray and beige to satisfy almost everyone, and it works with pretty much every style.

### 2. Move Away from the Walls

Rooms look larger if you place furniture toward the middle. Pulling the furniture away from the walls will make conversation areas more intimate and create a better sense of balance. Try putting a long table behind the sofa. Even in a small room, you can give the furnishings some space. It can be as simple as angling a chair or table slightly to add interest to the room. By moving the furniture even a little bit you might discover a fresh look for your space.

### 3. Carefully Size any Purchases

The phrase "measure twice, cut once" can also be phrased as, "measure twice, buy once" when designing. Measure and know the size of your room before you start to purchase furniture pieces. Take it a step further and put down some blue painter's tape to walk around the rug or furniture, checking the size before you purchase.

### 4. Decorate in Threes

The rule of three says that things arranged in odd numbers are more appealing, memorable, and effective than even-numbered groupings. Items to style as a trio include coffee table books, vases, or candles. Although three seems to be the "magic" number, you can decorate in groups of five or seven as well.

### 5. Lower the Artwork

Art can transform a space. According to designers, most people hang their art too high. Art should hang 60 to 62 inches from the floor. You want to keep your art at eye level. Also, do not feel like everything must hang at the same height. When hanging art and displaying décor, pair taller items with shorter ones, and switch up the placement on the walls.

## A GOOD STEAK DINNER

By now, you have unpacked, scrubbed, organized, and even decorated. It's time to relax and enjoy the feeling of home. I love a good steak dinner when celebrating a special occasion. With potatoes, a salad, and maybe a nice glass of red wine, you can toast to week one and take some time to appreciate the life ahead.

# Let's  Eat

## FIRST – SOME STEAK FACTS

**CUTS OF STEAK:**

There are dozens of cuts of beef, all with unique flavor profiles. The more you get to know beef — and the tastes of your family and friends — the further you can dive into customizing your preferred cuts. If you're a beginner, for best results choose beef of the highest quality. After you get more "seasoned" as a steak chef, you can experiment with different cuts and levels of quality.

 **Filet Mignon**
A tender steak with a mild flavor.
Serving size: 5-9 oz.

 **New York Strip**
This marbled steak is bone-in or boneless, with a firmer texture.
Serving size: 8-14 oz.

 **Top Sirloin**
A naturally lean cut.
Serving size: 5-10 oz.

 **Ribeye**
With the most marbling, this steak has the richest flavor.
Serving size: 8-14 oz.

 **T-Bone**
This is two steaks in one, a filet mignon and a NY strip with a "T" bone in the middle. Serving size: 12-18 oz. or more.

**ROOM TEMPERATURE:**

Whether in the freezer or refrigerator, bring your steak to room temperature before cooking. If it's frozen, thaw fully in the refrigerator and then place steaks on the kitchen counter. Season and let it rest 30 minutes before grilling.

## GRILLING THE PERFECT STEAK

When you're grilling steaks, heat matters. But it takes more than just getting the grill hot. Prepare your grill with variable heat sections: two burners on high and one on low if you're using gas, or a three-zone setup for charcoal grills.

Be sure the grates are hot before you place the steaks. Before adding any food to the grill, brush your clean grates with oil.

Place your steaks on the hot, oiled grates, directly over the heat source. The best thing to do for a steak on the grill is to leave it alone. Do not over-flip, press or poke. Flip it once when it is about 60% cooked. I call it the 60/40 rule, and it's going to help make sure your steak is evenly cooked. For total cooking times, look at each cut of meat and its thickness.

A perfectly grilled, flavorful steak has a crust on the outside and is juicy and tender inside. The "doneness" of a steak is determined by the internal temperature of the beef. Every steak eater has a preference, but most butchers will tell you medium-rare is the best. (However, it's always best to ask your dinner guests what they prefer.) Use a high-quality meat thermometer for reliable, accurate results.

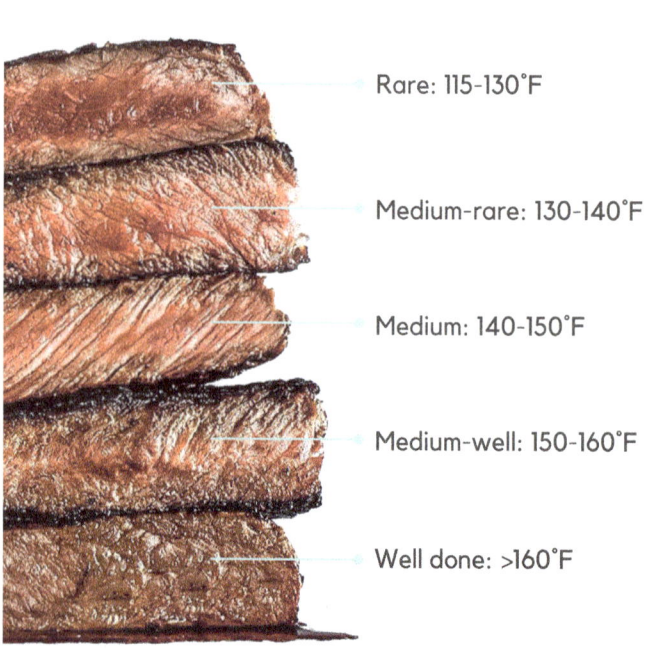

Rare: 115-130°F

Medium-rare: 130-140°F

Medium: 140-150°F

Medium-well: 150-160°F

Well done: >160°F

**Let your steak rest. This is essential.**

The best grillers take their steaks off the grill at five degrees below the target temperature. Then, let the steak sit. Bring it in and put a loose-fitting piece of tinfoil over the top. The steak's temperature will rise a few more degrees and the juices will redistribute throughout the meat.

When cutting steak, remember to cut against the grain. Cutting against the grain breaks up the muscle fibers and makes your steak more tender.

## STEAKS ON THE GRILL

There is no need to complicate things when it comes to seasonings. Simple sea salt and black pepper work great. If you feel adventurous, you can also try various steak seasonings or rubs. Always season at least 30 minutes before cooking so the flavors have time to work their way into the beef.

### INGREDIENTS:
Steaks - I like boneless ribeye (about 12 oz. each)
• OR •
Filet mignon (8 to 10 oz. each), trimmed
2 T. extra virgin olive oil
Sea salt
Freshly ground pepper

### DIRECTIONS:

Before grilling, remove the steaks from the refrigerator. Rub lightly with olive oil and season with salt and pepper. I also like to add some Weber® Chicago Steak® seasoning. Let sit, covered, at room temperature for 30 minutes.

Heat your grill on high (500 degrees if the grill has a gauge).

When hot, brush grates with oil and place the steaks on the grill. Cook until slightly charred. For a filet mignon, medium-rare, I cook about four to five minutes on the first side. (See the tips on previous pages.) Turn the steaks over one time and continue to grill for three minutes — checking the temperature (medium-rare = 130 to 140 degrees).

Let it rest. Transfer the steaks to a cutting board or platter, tent loosely with tinfoil, and let rest for five to ten minutes before serving.

## ROASTED GARLIC POTATOES

**INGREDIENTS:**

Potatoes (amount/guest)
1-2 garlic cloves, minced
Olive oil
Sea salt
Pepper

**DIRECTIONS:**

Wash the potatoes and dice them into 1-inch pieces. You can peel the potatoes or leave the skin on, it's your preference. (Potatoes will start to brown if left exposed to the open air. If you want to prep ahead of time, put the potatoes in water and drain when ready to cook.)

Preheat the oven to 425 degrees.

Put the potatoes into a bowl. Salt, pepper and drizzle with oil. Add minced garlic. Toss to mix. Place on a cookie sheet in single layer.

Bake for 30-40 minutes until golden brown. Stir occasionally.

## CRANBERRY WALNUT SALAD

### INGREDIENTS:

1 (5-7 oz. pkg.) mixed greens
1 cup dried sweetened cranberries
1 (4 oz. pkg.) feta cheese, crumbled
½ cup toasted walnuts, chopped
2 T. balsamic vinegar
1 T. honey
1 tsp. Dijon mustard
¼ tsp. pepper
¼ cup extra virgin olive oil
Fresh bread

### DIRECTIONS:

Whisk together vinegar, honey, mustard, and pepper in a small bowl. You can make this portion of the dressing ahead of time, and store it in the refrigerator until ready. Layer greens, cranberries, feta cheese, and walnuts in a shallow dish.

When ready, slowly add the oil to the dressing mixture in a thin stream, whisking constantly. Pour over the salad and toss gently. Serve with fresh bread. Enjoy.

Serves 4-6 people.

## STEWARDS OF THE HOUSE FOR NOW

By: Justine B.

My mom and I were outside looking at the plants in the yard of our new home, and she was telling me about each one. As she was describing each plant (she has more of a green thumb than I do), we noticed a car driving by very slowly, looking at the house.

I didn't think much of it at first. The prior owners mentioned that it was common for people to slow down to look at their beautiful yard and garden. But this car seemed different and eventually we waved, and they stopped to say hi.

The man driving was the grandson of the original builder who constructed the house in 1907. He and his wife lived in Indiana but happened to be in the area to buy a boat and wanted to drive by and see Grandpa Paul's old house. The grandson was blown away by the changes that had been made since he was last here as a kid, yet happy that it all still seemed so familiar: the bones, yard and setting.

*He said that Paul was the youngest of 11 children. He told us his grandfather's story and said that if we hear any ghosts around the house, it's probably just Paul trying to help us fix something.*

Both the family immediately prior to us and Paul's family provided glorious stories about our house. It was a wonderful blessing, something to remind us that at any address we are just stewards of the place for the time being. For us, the house at 2117 had a long life before us and will have a long life after us as well.

> The man driving was the grandson of the original builder...

# House Notes 8

ENTERTAINING TIPS

### 1. Lighten Up by Turning Down
If you can, turn the lights down a bit for evening dinners to make the mood more relaxing and restaurant-like. I love the look of candles on the table but don't want to burn my guests. Battery-operated candles have moving wicks and look fantastic on the table. Some have a remote control which makes it easy to "turn on" the table as people arrive.

### 2. Clearly Plated
Many people have beautiful, fine china for entertaining and special occasions. If you do, use it. If you don't, I recommend purchasing a stack of glass plates. I own 25 plates for big parties that cost only $2 each. They are easy to dress up and look fantastic for a dinner party during any season. To set the table, start with chargers or placemats and arrange the glass plates with folded napkins. It will look fancy without breaking the bank.

### 3. Cloth Napkins
I love cloth napkins to accent my table setting. Look for napkins that work all year around and are machine-washable. Check the fabric and washing instructions so you can clean the linens at home after a party. You can simply place the napkin on the plate or get fancy with folding ideas. (See the next page).

### 4. Water Ready
Years ago, I was at a restaurant and noticed the bottles they set on the table looked like sangria bottles from De La Costa. I bought the sangria and after enjoying it, removed the label and cleaned the interior. For dinner parties, I fill and refrigerate these glass bottles with water ahead of time and place them on the table, so guests have water refills during dinner.

### 5. Sound of Music
I love to have light jazz music playing for dinner parties. If you can, put the speaker in the next room so the music doesn't overpower the conversation.

## DINNER PARTY

Ideas for hosting the first dinner party in your new home.

# Let's  Eat

### FIRST — SOME TIPS ON SETTING THE TABLE

I love setting the table. Maybe it's because I can do it early and take my time. Maybe it's the anticipation of family and friends coming soon. I am not sure why, but for me, it is one of the most gratifying things about a special dinner.

There are countless ways to make your dinner table come alive, from napkin rings to floral arrangements. Your centerpiece should be low and small so guests don't have to look around it to talk to one another, and so you have maximum "real estate" for your food and place settings. Don't overthink the décor. A table runner and candles with the dishes and glassware is beautiful and, many times, enough.

Folded napkins make the table fun. Here are 12 folding ideas.
Search for each fold online to watch a tutorial.

Source: https://www.veranda.com/home-decorators/a28480947/napkin-folding/

# BEEF TENDERLOIN

## INGREDIENTS:

5 lb. tenderloin, trimmed
Olive oil
Steak seasoning
Garlic powder
Sea salt
Ground pepper
Fresh bread

## DIRECTIONS:

Remove meat from refrigerator and get to room temperature (about 3 hours). Cut off plastic wrap and rub the meat on all sides with oil and seasonings.

Preheat the oven to 425 degrees.

Place in a roasting pan with a grate on the bottom. Put a small amount of water in the bottom of the pan. Do not cover.

Cook for 40-50 minutes for medium-rare. (So much depends upon the oven so check the temperature with the thermometer. Try not to open the door before 40 minutes.) Get the center of the meat to 130-135 degrees.

Remove from the oven and tent. Then let stand for at least 20 minutes.

If your party is smaller, reduce the size of the tenderloin. A good rule of thumb is 4-8 oz. of meat per person depending on their appetite. For six people, a 2-3 lb. tenderloin will do. Make sure to adjust the cooking time based on the size of the tenderloin.

We love to serve with a sliced French baguette.

Serves 10-12 people depending on the thickness of the slices.

# FLAKY POTATOES

## INGREDIENTS:

2 lbs. frozen hash browns, thawed (shredded or cubed)
¼ tsp. pepper
1 tsp. salt
½ cup onion, chopped
1 can cream of mushroom soup
1 can cream of potato soup
8 oz. sour cream
8 oz. shredded cheddar cheese
¼ cup butter, melted
Corn Flakes

## DIRECTIONS:

This dish can be made ahead and put into the refrigerator until ready to cook. Preheat the oven to 350 degrees.

Mix all ingredients, except butter and Corn Flakes, in a large bowl. Spread into a 9x13 glass pan or a high-sided, white CorningWare® dish. Put 2 cups of Corn Flakes into a Ziplock® bag with ¼ cup of melted butter and crush into small pieces with your hands. Spread over the top of the potatoes.

Bake for 1 ½ hours. The potatoes will come out piping hot and hold the heat, so be careful when serving.

Serves 10-12 people.

## ROASTED BROCCOLI AND CAULIFLOWER

### INGREDIENTS:

4 cups broccoli florets (bite-size)
4 cups cauliflower florets (bite-size)
2 T. olive oil
1 clove garlic, minced
½ cup fresh Parmesan cheese, shredded
Salt & pepper to taste

### DIRECTIONS:

Preheat the oven to 450 degrees.

Rinse broccoli and cauliflower and pat dry. Cut pieces into uniform sizes. Put in large bowl and toss with oil and minced garlic. Spread on cooking sheet in single layer. Sprinkle with shredded Parmesan, so cheese gets into the crevices of the florets. Season with salt and pepper.

Roast 20 minutes, stirring halfway through, until vegetables are fork-tender yet still crisp.

Cook in the oven while the beef rests.

Serves 6-8 people.

# Good Story

## WRITE YOUR GOOD STORY

By: _____

> Now that you are settled, spend a moment to write your new home story.

# House Notes 9

## BACKYARD PARTY TIPS

Backyard parties are a relaxing, fun way to entertain. They are perfect for a new homeowner because the menu can be simple and yet entertain a crowd of any size. It also keeps the party outdoors and casual. People get to see your new home without making a mess inside.

### 1. Inviting the Guests

Determine the number of people you want at the party. Will you invite children? What time will you eat? Sending out invites for a casual party can be as easy as an email or text, but be sure to include key details like timing, theme, address, RSVP, etc.

### 2. Party Theme

Having a theme for the party can be fun. A beach party or backyard game theme can make party planning easier. Based on your theme, add a signature cocktail. You can find endless ideas for creative, tasty cocktails online (including "mocktails"), and if kids are invited, make sure you have something for them as well.

### 3. The Menu

Backyard parties offer an opportunity for a simple, casual menu. Think of dishes that can be made ahead of time, so you're not spending the day in the kitchen. Things like pasta salads, chips, and beans are easy to serve for large crowds. Check out the recipe ideas on the following pages.

### 4. Outdoor Ambiance

Use music and lighting to add to the fun atmosphere in the backyard. Tiki torches or simply strung lights can create a beautiful setting after dark. If your party does go past dusk, set out a few cans of mosquito repellant in case unwanted guests arrive.

### 5. Create a Relaxing Atmosphere

Backyard parties allow guests to stroll and talk. Set drinks and food on various tables around your deck, patio or yard. I love arranging the chairs in small groups so people can sit and talk to each other. Having a cornhole game, or other backyard game, is also a wonderful way to engage your guests.

## BACKYARD RECIPES TO FEED A CROWD

Start with some simple snacks for your guests to nibble on. Nuts can be placed throughout, along with a few easy appetizers. The grill is perfect to cook up a main course for the backyard. Add a couple easy sides and a drink, and you've got a great party!

# Let's Eat

## SALTY BEEF DIP

Dips — served with pretzels or crackers — give your guests something to nibble on as the party gets started. This is a favorite at our house at cocktail hour. Make the dip ahead of time and keep it covered in the fridge.

### INGREDIENTS:
2 (8 oz.) cream cheese
1 pkg. Buddig™ Beef (in a pouch, in the refrigerator section of the store)
1 cup green onion, sliced
1 ½ T. Ac'cent® flavor enhancer
1 ½ T. Worcestershire sauce
Splash of milk
Pretzels or crackers

### DIRECTIONS:
Let the cream cheese get to room temperature. Chop green onions with just a little of the "green" included. Chop the beef into tiny pieces. Mix all ingredients well in a bowl. Add a little milk if the mixture is too hard. Put into two small serving dishes, cover, and refrigerate.

Serve with pretzels or crackers. We love this with Wheat Thins or Crunchmaster® crackers.

# CHARCUTERIE BOARD

I LOVE a beautiful board of cheese and other grabbable snacks at a party. I sometimes cut out pictures and then try to replicate the look when entertaining.

The serving dish can be anything from a wooden cutting board to a tray. I love long wooden trays with small sides to keep things in place as people reach for a tasty treat.

It's important to offer a mixture of tastes and textures. That means things like cheese and grapes, crackers and nuts, or chocolates and olives. Mixing it up with different flavors creates an interesting look and satisfies a range of palates.

One tip: Add a few sprigs of rosemary or basil leaves to the board for a touch of green.

**INGREDIENT IDEAS:**
Sliced cheese — pepper jack or cheddar
Soft cheese — brie or goat milk
Chocolate almonds
Cashews
Sausage or meat sticks (cut into bite-size pieces)
Prosciutto
Kalamata olives (put in a little dish and place on the tray)
Thinly sliced apple
Sliced baguette bread
Cherry tomatoes
Sliced zucchini
Hummus
Crackers

## BRATS AND ONIONS

I love using the grill to serve a crowd. One Midwest favorite is bratwurst, a fresh link sausage that originated in Germany. Sheboygan-style bratwursts are a popular variation from Wisconsin, and I love Johnsonville® Original Brats. They're easy to eat in a casual atmosphere, like an outdoor patio or backyard.

### INGREDIENTS:
(Multiply for a crowd)

12 Johnsonville® Original Brats
1 large yellow onion
1 stick butter
Brat buns
Condiments
Old pan or pot you can put on the grill (or use a disposable foil lasagna pan)

### DIRECTIONS:

Cut onion into thin slices and put in a pan with chunks of butter. Get coals (or gas grill) hot and put the pan on the grill to cook the onions. Simultaneously put on a few brats, browning on both sides. Put the first round of cooked brats in the onion/butter mixture while cooking next round.

Rotate the brats from the grill to the pan of butter, letting them steep in the onions. Move the brats back and forth for about 30 minutes. Brats should be cooked and slightly charred. Keep adding to the pan until all the brats are cooked.

# LILY LAKE BEANS

It would not be brat night without a pot of Lily Lake Beans.
This recipe can easily be doubled for a large crowd.

## INGREDIENTS:

½ lb. ground beef
½ lb. bacon (if you don't eat pork, remove and add more beef)
1 T. Lipton® onion soup dry mix
1 (18 oz. jar) B&M® baked beans
1 (14 oz. can) butter beans

1 (14 oz. can) kidney beans
1 (14 oz. can) red beans
¾ cup brown sugar
1 T. white vinegar
½ cup ketchup
1 T. dry mustard

## DIRECTIONS:

Cook bacon until crispy and chop it into small pieces. Cook ground beef and drain well. Drain (do not rinse) beans and add to pot. Add all ingredients, mix well, and bring to a boil. Immediately turn down to simmer for 15-30 minutes. Can be made ahead and warmed up before dinner.

If you are serving a large crowd, put the beans in a crock pot on low. People can eat at their leisure and the beans will stay warm.

Serves 8-10 people.

### POOKY PASTA SALAD

This cold pasta is best if made early and allowed to steep in the dressing overnight.

#### INGREDIENTS:

1 lb. bag mixed bowtie pasta
1 bottle Girard's® Italian Dressing
1 can marinated artichoke hearts (drain well)
¼ lb. sundried tomatoes (drain oil from the jar, put tomatoes on a paper towel, and pat dry.)
1 cup sliced black olives
1 (2 oz. jar) pine nuts
¼ cup Parmesan cheese, grated

#### DIRECTIONS:

Cook bowtie pasta according to al dente directions. Drain and cool completely.

Mix in half a bottle of the dressing with cool pasta and add all other ingredients. Stir well. Chill in the refrigerator overnight. Just before serving, add more dressing to taste and top with grated cheese.

If you are serving outdoors in warm weather, put a bowl of ice under your serving bowl to keep the salad cool.

Serves 8-10 people.

# SPECIAL K® PEANUT BUTTER BARS

These are not only an absolute favorite of my kids but great for parties and events.

**INGREDIENTS:**

1 cup Karo® white syrup
1 cup sugar
1 cup peanut butter (creamy)
6 cups Special K® cereal
½ bag chocolate chips
½ bag butterscotch chips

**DIRECTIONS:**

Prep a 9x13 glass pan by rubbing bottom and sides with butter. Measure cereal into a large bowl and set aside. Put Karo® and sugar together in a pan and melt on the stove over medium heat, stirring constantly until clear. Add peanut butter and melt. Pour warm mixture over cereal and mix to coat. Press the mixture into a flat layer on the bottom of the glass pan. Cover your hand with a Ziplock® bag as you press.

Melt ½ bag chocolate chips and ½ bag butterscotch chips in the microwave for 1 minute 15 seconds. Place butterscotch on top as they melt slowly. Take out and stir. Depending on your microwave, you may need another 15 seconds to completely melt the mixture. Spread over the bars and let cool completely before cutting into squares.

These bars are delicious but might get soft in the sun. Serve them at the end of the meal or put them in the shade!

Serves 15 people or more depending on how big you cut them.

## MARGARITA HEAVEN

Even if you are serving beer and wine, a signature cocktail is fun at any party. Make sure to add a small, creative sign calling out your signature drink.

A pitcher of margaritas can be set with the other beverages. This simple recipe can be made ahead of time.

### INGREDIENTS:

1 can limeade, frozen
1 can Sprite®
1 bottle Corona® beer
Tequila

### DIRECTIONS:

Mix limeade and Sprite® in a pitcher. Fill the empty limeade can with tequila. Pour in Corona® and mix. Serve over ice.

Set the pitcher alongside stacked glasses and let guests pour their own.

## ENJOY YOUR NEW HOME

I sincerely hope this book has been a helpful and fun guide in what can be a chaotic time for you and your family while moving into a new home. But in the hustle and bustle, don't forget to take the time and pause to enjoy the small moments. Whether it's a kid picking up a paintbrush to help and dripping on the floor or furniture, or a delay with the moving truck that means you have to camp out in sleeping bags for the first night. Before you know it, 20 years will go by, and you'll still talk about those paint spills, the family campout in the living room, and the inconveniences of today will be the memories you cherish tomorrow.

*Pause, savor, and enjoy each moment in this new life point...*

## WELCOME HOME

*from Good Stories Publishing*

Being good is purposeful.

This book is from Good Stories Publishing, a story creator focusing on content that creates positivity in the universe. Good Stories authors value good things and want to create positive vibes.

We believe in good. By actively delivering positive stories, we are creating better lives, better families, and a better world.

*Tell us your Good Story*

We love to hear good stories.
**Share your story on the Good Stories social media platforms or our website at www.goodstoriespublishing.com**

# ABOUT THE AUTHOR

Marlene Byrne

Marlene is not a chef. She is not a television personality. She didn't star in a movie before deciding to bring you into her kitchen. She doesn't grow organic herbs. These recipes are not her creation but rather handed down from friends and family.

She is a Midwest mother whose extended family loves to get together to eat, laugh, and reminisce. Whose kids are growing up, moving out, and yet coming back.

She is also a writer. Marlene has written five children's books about backyard games under the umbrella of Project Play Books. She has also written novels based on inspirational true stories: *Music Has Legs* and *Do Not Discard*.

This time, she wanted to write a book that would share recipes and stories with readers and help people with tips that could make their lives better. *Welcome Home* is meant to help new homeowners in a time of transition and make the journey less stressful and more fun.

*"I love to entertain so I wrote this book to give families easy ideas that would make their gatherings fun and memorable. Many of the good stories and tips in my books come from my readers and fans. I want to be a conduit for sharing ideas that make families happy."*

Marlene Byrne

Find other books from author Marlene Byrne at www.marlenebyrne.com.

**Life Point Books**

**ABOUT LIFE POINT BOOKS™:**

The Life Point Books™ series focuses on celebrating the milestones of our lives. Our books are meant to be simple with recipes to feed your family but not break your budget. The ingredients are easily found at your local grocery store. The tips are meant as reminders to make your home life better and keep you safe.
Most importantly, these everyday ideas are meant to be shared.

www.ingramcontent.com/pod-product-compliance
Lightning Source LLC
Chambersburg PA
CBHW080606170426
43209CB00007B/1344